CONTENTS

DRAGON BONES

Have you ever wondered where the storytellers from ancient civilizations got their ideas about fire-breathing dragons? Perhaps their ideas came from the discovery of fossilized dinosaur bones unearthed thousands of years ago. Many people believed the dinosaur bones belonged to terrible dragon lizards. Even today, people are still intrigued by dinosaur remains and want to know more about the dinosaur age.

Only rarely are dinosaur skeletons found complete, like the skeleton of this plant-eating sauropod found on the west slope of the Rocky Mountains.

Stories of dragons are often told by actors wearing frightening masks.

PALEONTOLOGY PUZZLES

Scientists who study fossils and dinosaur remains are called paleontologists. They attempt to explain what dinosaurs looked like, how they lived, and when and why dinosaurs became extinct. A paleontologist's work is like putting together a giant jigsaw puzzle with many missing pieces.

Each layer of exposed rock (or strata) in a canyon may contain fossils. A layer containing dinosaur bones is called a "dinosaur fossil record."

Giant dragonflies with two-foot wingspans left fossil remains as proof that giant insects existed during the dinosaur age.

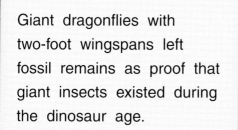

This fossilized shell belonged to an extinct sea creature called an ammonite. Scientists believe that ammonites became extinct at about the same time that dinosaurs became extinct.

LINKS TO ANCIENT LIFE

More than 350 species of dinosaur fossils have been found. Based on studies of these fossils, scientists conclude that plant-eating sauropods, like buffalo, grazed together in herds, and that meat-eating theropods hunted together in packs, like wolves. Other types of animals lived with the dinosaurs, too. Some species from the dinosaur age still live today, while other species vanished along with the dinosaurs.

The diplodocus – a sauropod – was so heavy that the ground shook when it walked. Scientists believe that sauropods fed on ancient coniferous plants. Their well-worn teeth suggest that tree tops were a favorite food item.

Giant swimming reptiles called mosasaurs ruled the seas. They fed on ammonites. Diving birds called hesperornises lived along inland seas.

Flying reptiles called pterosaurs soared overhead.

END OF THE DINOSAURS

Why did dinosaurs and other large reptiles and lizards disappear, while the smaller reptiles, amphibians, birds, and mammals survived? Scientists are investigating many possibilities. Here are some of their theories.

Theory One

Meteors crashed into Earth, causing fireballs that burned forests, depleting the food source of sauropods. Smoke in the atmosphere from the burning forests caused the climate to cool. At the same time, increased volcanic activity poured ash into the atmosphere, adding to the problems.

Theory Two

The climate gradually became cooler as land masses divided into new continents. The dinosaurs had no protection against the cold winters.

Theory Three

By spreading pollen, insects helped flowering plants spread over the landscape. These plants overtook a critical food supply of the sauropods – the coniferous forests. Many sauropods starved to death. Fierce meat-eating theropods, which depended on the sauropods for food, soon faced extinction as well.

Theory Four

Mammals migrated across land bridges between colliding continents. They carried new diseases against which the dinosaurs had no natural resistance.

Amphibians are survivors from the dinosaur age. Why did they survive? Some scientists believe that the aquatic habitats of amphibians may have spared them from the temperature extremes believed to have killed the dinosaurs. They know, too, that amphibians have a winning tactic in the battle for survival. Heavy losses to predators are offset by the large number of eggs each female lays.

Yet today, amphibian populations are declining because of deforestation, loss of wetlands, acid rain, and increased ultraviolet light levels. Some scientists think that similar factors slowly brought dinosaurs to extinction.

Amphibians, such as this toad, are predators. They eat dozens of insects every day. Perhaps they survived because their food source remained plentiful.

Eryops was a giant amphibian. It became extinct, but many amphibians survived.

Poison glands in the skins of red-spotted newts provide protection from predators. This trait could have allowed them to survive through the dinosaur age.

REPTILES – SURVIVORS

Scientists who study reptiles believe many of today's lizards provide clues as to what dinosaurs looked like and how they behaved. We know that reptiles lay hard-shelled eggs on land. This gives them the freedom to explore and live in environments outside the aquatic habitats of amphibians. They also depend on heat from the sun and their environment to maintain body heat.

Komodo dragons are the largest lizards living in our modern world. They lay their eggs in underground nests in the jungles of Indonesia.

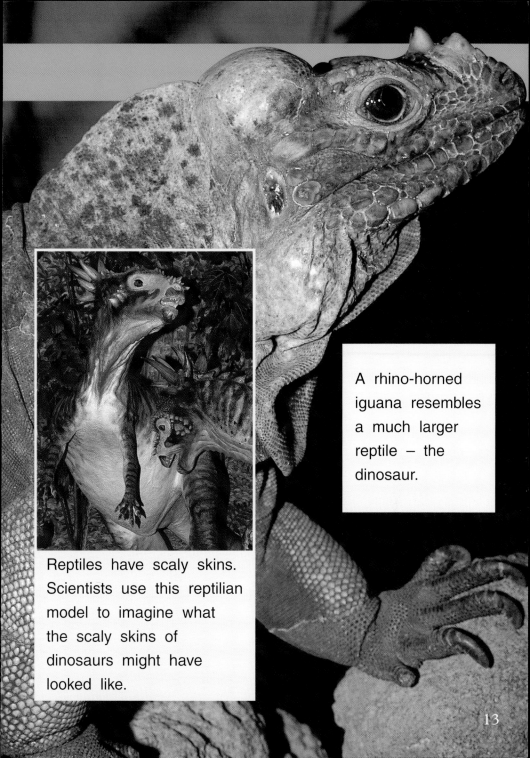

A rhino-horned iguana resembles a much larger reptile – the dinosaur.

Reptiles have scaly skins. Scientists use this reptilian model to imagine what the scaly skins of dinosaurs might have looked like.

Fossils of baby maiasaurs found in nests show that they received food from a caring mother who shared a rookery with other watchful mothers. Scientists believe many dinosaurs had strong maternal instincts.

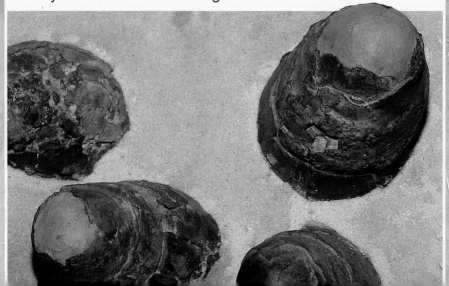

A cold-blooded Cuban crocodile is panting through its open jaws to cool off on a hot summer day. Scientists study the metabolisms of reptiles to learn how changing climates might have affected the dinosaurs. The sex of some reptiles is determined by egg temperature. A population of all male (or all female) dinosaurs would have quickly become extinct.

A young alligator warms up in the morning sun. Scientists debate how dinosaurs may have regulated their body heat. Energetic predators such as theropods may have been warm-blooded. Slower moving sauropods were probably cold-blooded and used their gigantic body mass to store heat.

15

BIRDS – SURVIVORS

Scientists believe that birds may be close relatives of the meat-eating dinosaurs – the theropods. Warm-blooded metabolisms and an ability to fly may have provided birds with some advantages in the struggle for survival. Birds, like dinosaurs, lay eggs. But the dinosaur connection goes further. Great numbers of dinosaurs congregated in nesting areas for safety from predators. Many birds do the same thing.

Scientists are learning that the parenting behaviors of some modern birds and dinosaurs are very similar. By studying birds, scientists are better able to understand dinosaurs.

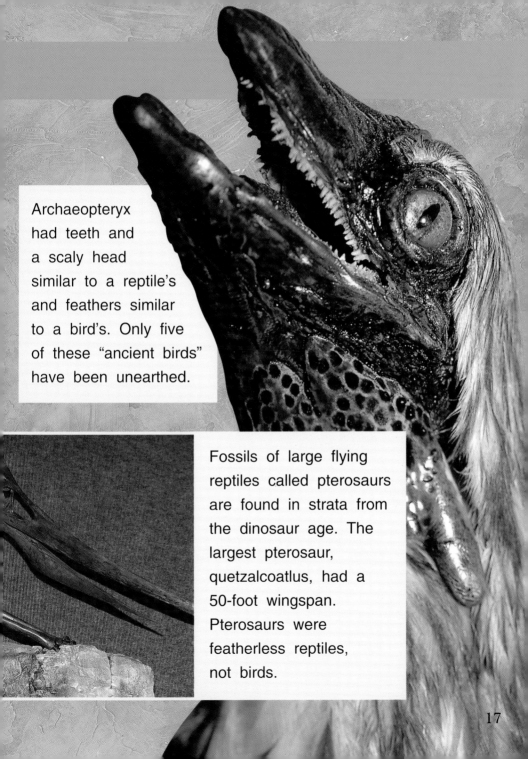

Archaeopteryx had teeth and a scaly head similar to a reptile's and feathers similar to a bird's. Only five of these "ancient birds" have been unearthed.

Fossils of large flying reptiles called pterosaurs are found in strata from the dinosaur age. The largest pterosaur, quetzalcoatlus, had a 50-foot wingspan. Pterosaurs were featherless reptiles, not birds.

This great blue heron feeds a youngster that is almost old enough to fly. Scientists have found fossil evidence suggesting that some dinosaurs behaved similarly.

The head of this immature white ibis is covered with scales. This suggests to scientists that birds, reptiles, and dinosaurs are related!

Two great egrets build a nest from sticks.

Like modern birds, duckbilled dinosaurs such as this hypacrosaurus built nests from dead vegetation.

CONCLUSION

Dinosaurs lived on Earth for 165 million years. Today, 65 million years later, few creatures excite our imagination as much as the dinosaurs. As scientists search to piece together a complete picture of dinosaurs and the age in which they lived, we discover new connections to life on Earth today.

The tuatara's ancestors trod the earth more than 225 million years ago. Today, the tuatara is often called the "living fossil."

INDEX

ABOUT THE AUTHOR

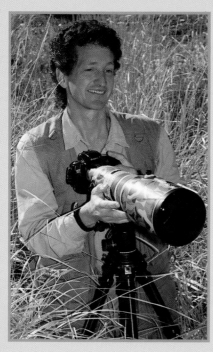

Buck Wilde's work as a naturalist and a wildlife photographer has taken him all around the world. In *The Dinosaur Connection*, however, he travels back in time to look at life in the dinosaur age. Through the lens of his camera, he documents evidence of the dinosaurs and ancient flying reptiles and sea-going lizards. Then, using his extensive knowledge of today's natural world, he draws the connection between the dinosaur age and our own.

Who Knows?

Written by **Buck Wilde**
Photographed by **Buck Wilde**
Illustrated by **Bryan Pollard** and **Paul Rogers** (background)
Additional photography by **Key-Light Image Library:** (dinosaur skeleton, cover; p. 21); **Photobank Image Library:** (p. 20); **Superstock Photo Library:** (p. 3)

05 04 03 02 01 00
10 9 8 7 6 5 4 3 2

Published in the United States by

a division of Reed Elsevier Inc.
500 Coventry Lane
Crystal Lake, IL 60014

Printed in Hong Kong
ISBN: 0-7901-1878-5